The Usborne Book of
ART
Skills

Fiona Watt

Designed and illustrated by Antonia Miller,
Katrina Fearn, Natacha Goransky and Vici Leyhane

Additional illustrations by Felicity House and Jan McCafferty
Photographs by Howard Allman

For links to more art activities online,
go to www.usborne.com/quicklinks and
enter the title of this book.

Contents

Materials

The techniques in this book use materials which can be found in art supply and craft stores. These two pages give information on some of the materials and how to use them.

Paint

The types of paint used in this book are watercolor paint, acrylic paint, poster paint and gouache.

You can buy watercolor paints in tubes or in solid blocks called pans. Mix the paints with water before you use them.

Gouache and poster paints are quite thick and opaque. They can be used without mixing with water.

Acrylic paints come in tubes or bottles. Squeeze them onto an old plate or palette. You can add water to make them thinner and more transparent.

This dog was painted with acrylic paint. See page 67 for this technique.

Pastels

In the book, there are several techniques which use oil pastels or chalk pastels. These are usually sold in sets.

Wax crayons can be substituted for oil pastels. They are good for rubbing and resist techniques.

Oil pastels

Oil pastels give a brighter effect than chalk pastels. Chalk pastels are good for techniques where colors are blended.

You'll find this scratched pastel technique on page 88.

Chalk pastels

4

Inks

Some of the ideas use colored inks, which come in bottles. You can also use the ink from a pen cartridge.

Pens

You'll also need a pen for some of the techniques. Felt-tip pens with permanent ink are ideal as they don't bleed, and they draw on top of most surfaces, including acrylic paint.

Permanent felt-tip pens are available in different colors and thickness.

Paper

Under the heading of each project there is a suggestion for the type of paper to use. The examples are shown at their real size unless you're told to use another size of paper.

Thick watercolor paper that is 190gsm (90lb) or above won't wrinkle too much when you paint on it.

Hot-pressed watercolor paper has the smoothest surface. Rough watercolor paper has the most texture.

Bristol paper comes in pads or as individual sheets. It will wrinkle when you paint on it.

Different types of paper, such as colored writing paper, textured paper and old magazines are used for the techniques in this book.

Tissue paper flowers

BRISTOL PAPER OR THIN WHITE CARDBOARD

 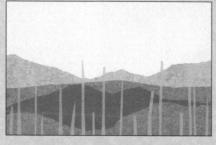 

1. Rip some strips of blue tissue paper. Glue them across a piece of paper, making them overlap.

2. Cut some thin strips of green tissue paper for the stems and glue them at the bottom of the paper.

3. Cut out some red petals. Glue four petals around the top of some of the stems.

4. Cut out some orange petals. Glue them around other stems, overlapping some of the red petals.

5. Use a thin felt-tip pen to draw a line around each petal. It doesn't need to be too accurate.

6. Draw a small circle in the middle of each flower, then add two or three lines to each petal.

These flowers also have outlines drawn along their stems.

Reflections in water

GRAY OR ANOTHER PALE COLOR OF PAPER

1. Cut a large rectangle of gray paper, then fold it in half with its long sides together. Crease the fold then open the paper.

2. Use a white oil pastel to draw three thick lines above the fold. Draw lots of buildings, trees, street lights, a moon and stars.

3. Fold the paper again, then rub all over it with the back of a spoon. This transfers your drawing to the other half.

4. Open the paper. Paint the top half of the picture with dark blue ink or watercolor paint. The pastel will resist the paint.

5. Mix some water with the same color and paint it below the fold. Brush darker lines on top to make it look like water.

6. When it's dry, draw over the moon and lights with a yellow pastel. Fold the paper and rub over it to make yellow reflections.

Simple figures
THICK BRIGHT PAPER OR CARDBOARD

1. Cut a piece of thick paper or cardboard. Rip a rectangle from some brown butcher paper and glue it in the middle.

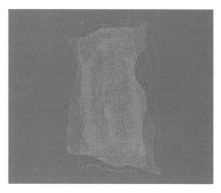

2. Rip a slightly wider rectangle from a bright piece of tissue paper and glue it over the brown butcher paper.

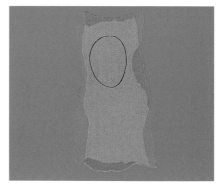

3. When the glue has dried, use a water-based felt-tip pen or a fountain pen to draw an oval for the face.

4. Draw two lines for the neck and a round-necked T-shirt. Add lines for the arms, but don't worry about drawing hands.

5. Draw a curved line for the eyebrow and nose, then add the other eyebrow and eyes. Draw the ears, hair and lips.

6. Then, dip a paintbrush into some clean water. Paint the water along some of the lines to make the ink run a little.

7. Rip a rough T-shirt shape from tissue paper and glue it over your drawing. Add a torn paper stripe, too.

8. Finally, when the glue has dried, paint thin stripes across the T-shirt using a bright color of watercolor paint.

Fantasy castle
BRISTOL PAPER OR THIN CARDBOARD

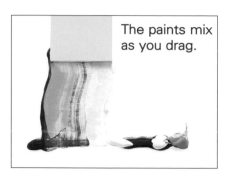

The paints mix as you drag.

1. Squeeze a line of acrylic paint along the bottom of the paper, straight from the tube. Use blue, turquoise and white.

2. Cut pieces of thick cardboard, making them different widths. Place a piece below the paint, then drag it upward.

3. Then, use the other pieces of cardboard to drag more towers, making them different heights. Leave it to dry.

4. Put some black paint onto a plate and dip the edge of another piece of cardboard into it. Drag it over the dried paint.

5. Dip the edge of the cardboard into the black paint again and use it to print lines for bridges between the towers.

6. Dip a narrow piece of cardboard into the paint. Drag small rectangles under the towers, to give them shadows.

7. When the paint has dried, use a black felt-tip pen to draw bridges, trees, turrets, windows and weather vanes.

This sunset scene was created using the same technique.

Small birds were drawn
around these towers to
give the towers a
sense of scale.

Tissue paper fruit

TISSUE PAPER

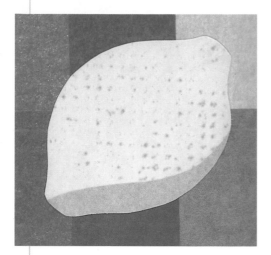

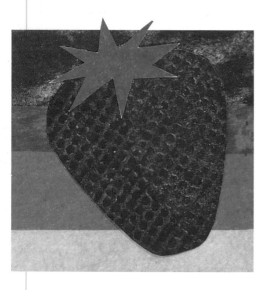

Try using different sides of the grater to get different textures.

Orange

1. Cut a circle from orange tissue paper. Then, cut a curved strip of tissue paper and glue it along one side.

2. Lay the tissue paper orange on a grater. Then, rub the side of an orange oil pastel or wax crayon gently over the paper.

Apple

3. Continue rubbing until the orange is covered with texture. Then, use a fine black felt-tip pen to add a stalk to the top.

Cut an apple shape from green tissue paper. Rub it with a green pastel around one side and at the top. Glue on a stalk.

Lemon

Cut a lemon from yellow tissue paper. Glue a green strip along one edge. Rub it with a yellow oil pastel, then a light green one.

Lime

Cut the shape of a lime from green tissue paper. Add a green strip along one edge, then rub it all over with a green pastel.

14

This background was made by overlapping rectangles of tissue paper.

Strawberry

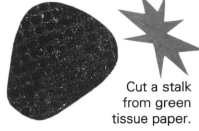

Cut a stalk from green tissue paper.

Cut a strawberry from red tissue paper. Add a red strip covering about half of the shape. Rub it with a yellow oil pastel.

Grapefruit

Cut a circle from yellow tissue paper and add a pale green strip. Rub it with a yellow, then a light green pastel. Add a stalk.

Pear

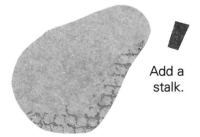

Add a stalk.

Cut a pear shape from green tissue paper. Rub down one side with a green pastel. Then, glue on a stalk.

Printed birds in a tree

ANY TYPE OF THICK PAPER

1. For the branches, pour some brown poster paint onto an old plate, then dip the edge of a strip of thick cardboard into it.

2. Press the painted edge onto your paper. Dip the cardboard into the paint, then print another branch, joining the first one.

The bodies and heads of these birds were printed at different angles to make them look animated.

You don't need this half.

3. Dip different widths of cardboard into the paint and print more branches. Leave spaces between them for the birds.

4. While the branches are drying, cut a small potato in half, lengthways. Then, cut one piece in half again.

5. For the birds' bodies, spread red paint on some paper towels. Press the cut side of one of the pieces of potato onto it.

6. Print a body onto the paper, with the straight edge at the top. Print more bodies in the spaces between the branches.

7. For the tails, dip the edge of some cardboard into the paint. Put it at the end of the body and twist it. Fingerprint the heads.

8. For the wings, cut a slice off the other small piece of potato. Press it in orange paint and print it on the body.

9. Paint a yellow beak and a blue eye on each bird. Then, paint short yellow lines for the legs, using a thin brush.

Paper shapes

ANY KIND OF COLORED PAPER

Spiral

1. Cut a circle from colored paper, then draw a spiral from the edge of the circle to the middle of it.

2. At the middle of the circle, curve the line around a little, then draw another line out to the edge of the circle.

3. Cut along one of the lines of the spiral, turning the paper as you cut. Continue cutting until you reach the edge again.

Build up layers of different shapes on top of each other.

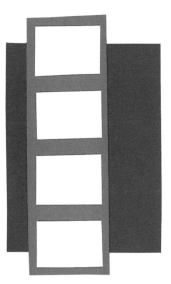

4. Cut the pointed end off the spiral and trim any wobbly bits from around the edges. Glue it onto another color of paper.

For a sun, cut a circle, then cut small triangles out of its edge. Glue another circle on top.

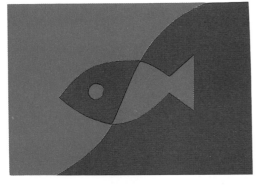

Fish

The shapes below could be used on a Valentine's card.

1. Cut two rectangles, the same size, from blue and orange paper. Then, draw a wavy line across the blue one.

2. Draw a simple outline of a fish across the line. Cut along the line, then cut out the front part of the fish, like this.

Try combining rounded shapes with squares and rectangles.

3. Glue the front part onto the orange rectangle. Then, cut out the back of the blue fish and glue it on. Glue on a blue eye.

Techniques for trees

The next four pages show you lots of different ways of drawing, painting and printing trees. When you try any of these techniques, you will get a better result if you make your tree bigger than the ones shown.

This oil painting of olive trees, by Vincent van Gogh, was painted in 1889. Van Gogh used lots of short lines to build up the shape and color of the trees and the sky.

Oil pastel trees

1. Draw a twisted tree trunk using dark brown oil pastels. Add several short branches.

2. Draw lots of short diagonal lines with a green oil pastel, overlapping the branches.

This tree was filled in with dots, instead of short lines.

3. Add more diagonal lines for the leaves, using a lighter green and a lime green pastel.

Use orange, brown and rusty pastels for fall leaves on a tree.

Pen and ink

1. Use brown ink to paint a very simple trunk with three thick branches coming from it.

2. Use green ink to paint a wavy line for the top of the tree. Then fill it in, leaving some small gaps.

3. Use a felt-tip or an ink pen to draw loopy lines around the edge of the tree and around the gaps.

Brushed branches

1. Paint a patch of green and brown watercolor paint. Splatter it by flicking the bristles of your brush.

2. Leave it to dry, then use different shades of brown watercolor paint to paint the trunk.

3. While the trunk is still wet, paint the branches by brushing the paint up onto the leaves.

Chalk pastel leaves

1. Paint a trunk with yellowy-brown watercolor paint. Add some branches, too.

2. Draw lines using a light green chalk pastel. Add some darker green lines on top.

3. Gently rub the tip of your little finger down the lines to smudge the chalks together.

More techniques for trees

Sponged leaves

Use a natural sponge if you have one.

1. Use the tip of a brush to paint the trunk and twisted branches of a tree, using watercolor paint or ink.

2. Dampen a piece of sponge, then dip it into some red paint. Dab it gently around the tops of the branches.

3. Wash the sponge, then squeeze as much water out as you can. Dip it into purple paint, then dab it around the branches.

This tree was blow-painted through a straw (see pages 56-57). Use this technique for a tree in winter.

Dip the hard end of a paintbrush in paint, then drag it across a patch of wet watercolor paint to make branches.

The leaves on this tree were printed with an eraser which had been cut into leaf shapes (see page 48 for this technique).

Zigzag trees

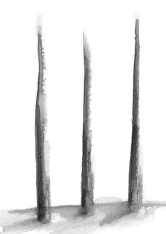

Use the tip of the brush.

1. Paint three tree trunks using green watercolor paint. Make them get thinner toward the top. Add some ground.

2. Put the tip of your brush at the top of a tree and paint a zigzag down the trunk. Make it get wider as you paint.

3. Continue painting, but leave part of the trunk showing at the bottom. Then, zigzag some clean water over the top.

Draw a trunk with brown chalk pastels. Scribble pastels for the leaves. Smudge them in a few places.

This stylized tree was drawn with chalk pastels. The leaves were drawn first then the trunk was added.

These leaves were painted first in dark green acrylic, then lighter green was added on top.

Sponge-printed snails
ANY TYPE OF PAPER

This is the end you print with.

1. Cut a piece of kitchen sponge 6½ x 1½ in. and two pieces 6 x 1in. Lay them together, matching the top edges, like this.

2. Cut a long piece of tape, so that it is ready to use. Fold the end of the long piece of sponge over the end of the shorter pieces.

3. Roll up the pieces of sponge carefully but not too tightly, keeping the edges even. Secure the sponge with the tape.

4. Pour blue acrylic paint onto an old plate and spread it a little. Then, dip the end of the sponge into the paint.

5. Print spirals all over a piece of paper. Press the sponge into the paint again each time you print a spiral.

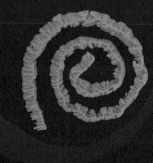

6. When the paint is dry, paint a snail's body below each spiral. Then, use a thin paintbrush to paint the antennae.

Paint small lines in
a curved trail
behind each snail.

The plants in this picture were
printed with pieces of cardboard,
cut into simple leaf shapes.

25

Fingerpainted flowers

BRISTOL PAPER OR THIN CARDBOARD

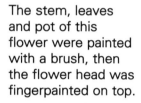

The stem, leaves and pot of this flower were painted with a brush, then the flower head was fingerpainted on top.

Drag your finger toward the middle each time.

1. Use a brush to paint a vase using poster paint or acrylic paint. When the paint is dry, fingerpaint some dots on the vase.

2. For a daffodil, dip a fingertip in yellow paint. Then, drag six lines for the petals, making them join in the middle.

3. Do several more daffodils above the vase. When the paint is dry, fingerpaint a star shape in the middle of the petals.

4. For a tulip, fingerpaint a curved line with bright red paint. Do another line that meets the first one at the bottom.

5. For the blue flowers, dip a fingertip in paint and print a small dot. Add lots more dots in a rough triangular shape.

6. To complete the flower arrangement, use a paintbrush to paint green leaves in the spaces between the flowers.

The yellow background in this picture was painted first, with a gap left for the vase. The vase was painted overlapping the yellow slightly.

Oil pastel lizards

ANY THICK WHITE PAPER

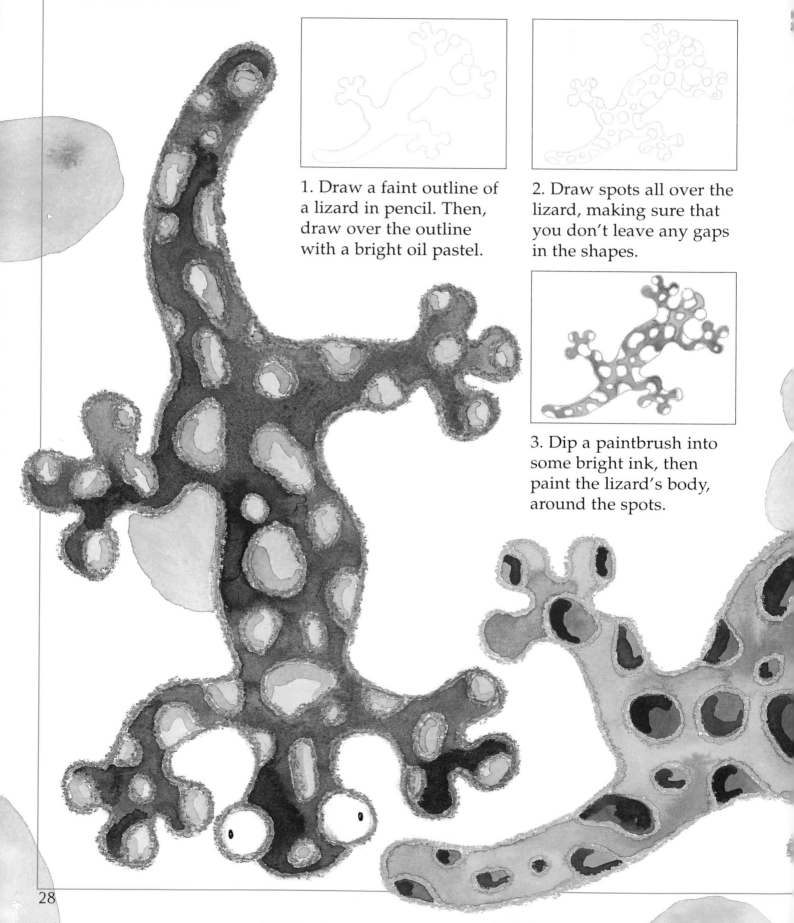

1. Draw a faint outline of a lizard in pencil. Then, draw over the outline with a bright oil pastel.

2. Draw spots all over the lizard, making sure that you don't leave any gaps in the shapes.

3. Dip a paintbrush into some bright ink, then paint the lizard's body, around the spots.

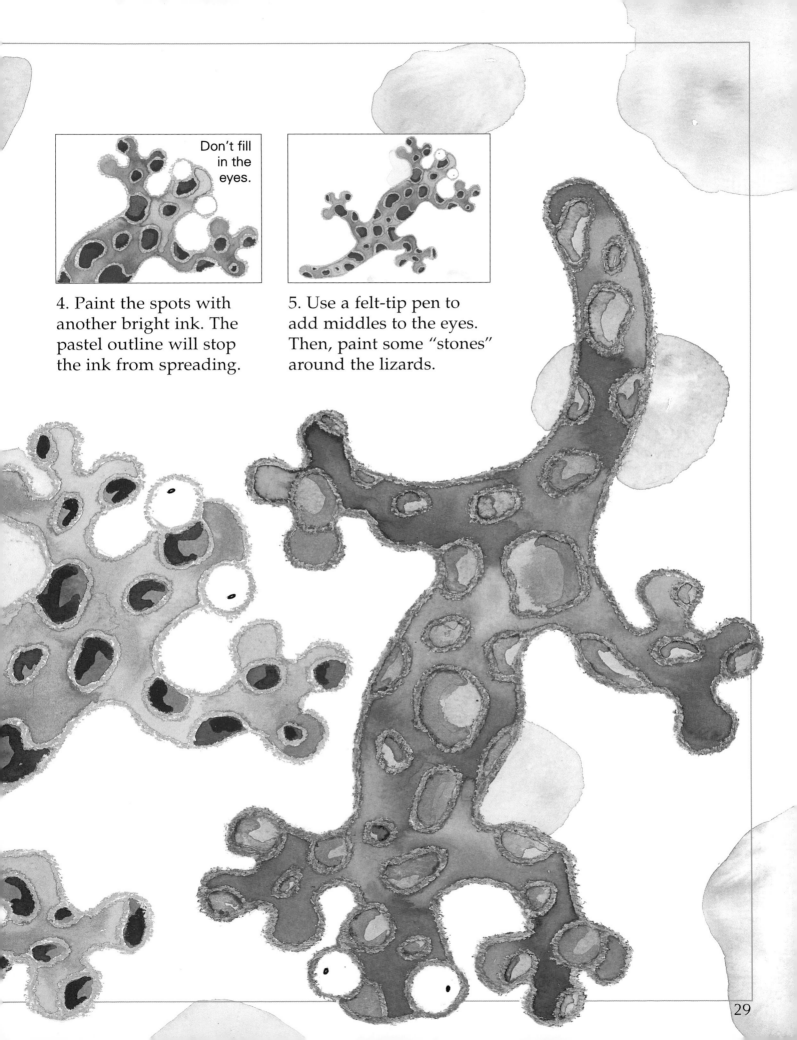

Don't fill in the eyes.

4. Paint the spots with another bright ink. The pastel outline will stop the ink from spreading.

5. Use a felt-tip pen to add middles to the eyes. Then, paint some "stones" around the lizards.

Textured houses

THICK WHITE CARDBOARD

1. Cut a zigzag at one end of a strip of cardboard. Then, paint a rectangle of acrylic paint on another piece of cardboard.

2. Drag the zigzag end of the cardboard across the paint again and again to make textured lines. Leave the paint to dry.

3. Cut several small triangles into the end of another cardboard strip. Drag it across another rectangle of paint.

4. For a very fine texture, drag the end of an old toothbrush across a rectangle of paint, again and again.

5. Do some more textured patches of paint by experimenting with different shapes cut into strips of cardboard.

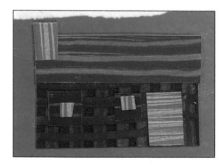

6. Cut rectangles from the textures for the buildings, windows, doors and roofs. Glue them on another piece of cardboard.

Patterned reptiles

BRISTOL PAPER OR WATERCOLOR PAPER

Instead of painting patterns, you could paint tiny triangles along the back and tail of the reptile.

1. Use ink to paint a body. Then, without lifting the brush, use less and less pressure, to paint a curling tail.

2. Dip the brush in the ink again and paint a head and a front and back leg. Add three "fingers" to each leg.

Paint a blue dot in the eye.

3. When the ink is dry, add green poster paint dots to the body and let them dry. Then, add little yellow dots on top.

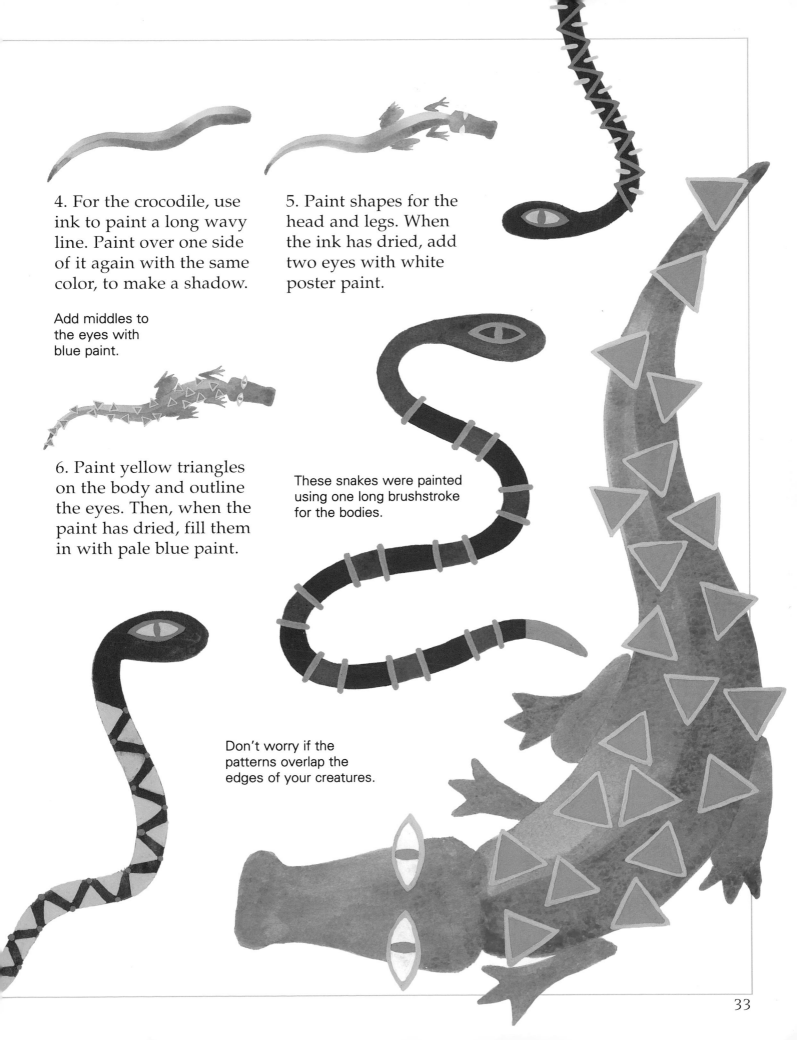

4. For the crocodile, use ink to paint a long wavy line. Paint over one side of it again with the same color, to make a shadow.

Add middles to the eyes with blue paint.

6. Paint yellow triangles on the body and outline the eyes. Then, when the paint has dried, fill them in with pale blue paint.

5. Paint shapes for the head and legs. When the ink has dried, add two eyes with white poster paint.

These snakes were painted using one long brushstroke for the bodies.

Don't worry if the patterns overlap the edges of your creatures.

33

Techniques for skies

On the next four pages you will find different techniques and tips for drawing and painting skies and clouds. Watercolor paints are very good for creating atmospheric skies.

This picture, called *Rain, Steam and Speed*, was painted in oil paints by J.M.W. Turner in 1844. The sky is stormy, but Turner painted bright areas on some of the clouds, which makes it look as if the sun is about to break through.

Watery clouds

1. Brush clean water onto a piece of watercolor paper. Then, use the tip of a brush to blob on patches of blue watercolor paint.

2. The paint will run. Then, press the brush a little bit more firmly in some places to make darker patches of sky.

Summer sky

1. Mix enough cobalt blue watercolor paint to cover a piece of watercolor paper. Paint a stripe across the top.

2. Paint another stripe below the first one before it has had a chance to dry. Paint quickly and make the stripes overlap.

3. Continue painting overlapping stripes all the way down the paper. This technique is known as 'painting a wash'.

4. Before the paint has dried, scrunch up a paper towel and dab it in several areas on the paper to lift some paint off.

5. When the paint has dried, mix some darker blue. Paint it along the bottom of each cloud to make shadows.

More techniques for skies

Rainy sky

1. Wet some watercolor paper with clean water. Then, mix Prussian blue watercolor paint with brown to make dark gray.

2. Paint overlapping stripes across the top of the paper. They don't need to be even or to start in the same place.

3. While the paint is still quite wet, add blue stripes across the middle, then gray ones at the bottom of the paper.

4. Before the paint has dried, swipe a cotton swab across the paint so that the bottom is almost white. Leave it to dry.

5. While it is drying, practice painting some fine lines for the rain, using gray paint on a piece of scrap paper.

6. When your painting is completely dry, paint fine lines for the rain, coming from the gray area near the top of the paper.

Starry night

1. Paint a piece of cardboard with dark blue acrylic paint. Move the brush around in a circle to get an uneven finish.

2. When the paint is dry, paint some planets with pale yellow acrylic paint. Then, add several stars around them.

3. For the tiny stars, dip a paintbrush into the yellow paint, then splatter it all over, following the steps on page 73.

Leaf collage
THICK PAPER OR CARDBOARD

1. Use dark paint and a thick paintbrush to paint vertical and horizontal lines on your paper.

2. When the paint has dried, cut a piece of tissue paper to cover the lines, and glue it on.

3. Rip some squares and rectangles from different colors of tissue paper and glue them on.

4. Cut a square of corrugated cardboard. Press it into some paint and print it several times.

5. Either cut out leaves from a picture in a magazine, or cut some leaf shapes from paper.

6. Cut small rectangles from a magazine picture of leaves or grass. Glue them on.

7. Add some horizontal and vertical lines with a felt-tip pen. Then, outline the leaves, loosely.

Doodle painting
BROWN BUTCHER PAPER

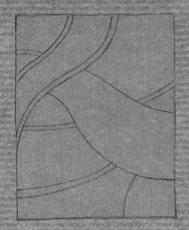

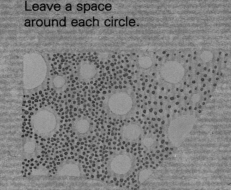

Leave a space around each circle.

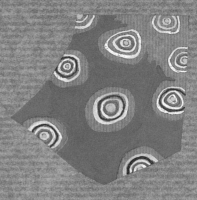

1. Use a pencil to draw a rectangle on some brown butcher paper. Draw curving lines to separate the rectangle into sections.

2. In one section, paint pale blue spots a little way apart. Fill in the spaces around them with lots of darker blue dots.

3. Paint white circles, one inside another. Add purple, blue and yellow inside them. Fill around the circles in light blue.

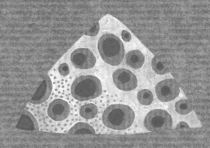

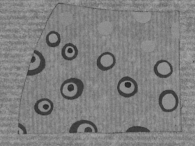

4. Fill one section with blue. When it's dry, add purple spots, then paint yellow and light blue circles around them.

5. In another section, paint blue spots. Fill in around them with white paint, leaving a space. Add tiny blue dots.

6. Paint light blue spots. Outline them in darker blue, then add a purple dot. Add a circle of pale blue dots around each one.

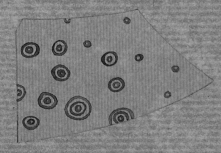

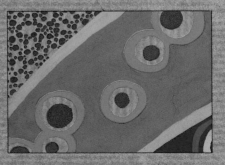

7. Use the tip of a thin brush to paint small purple circles. Paint more circles around them, leaving gaps in between.

8. Then, fill in the spaces between the circles with curved lines, following the shapes of the circles, like this.

9. Fill in the rest of the sections with different patterns of circles, spots and dots. Fill in thick lines between some sections.

41

Random patterns
THICK BRISTOL OR WATERCOLOR PAPER

1. Mix different colors of watercolor paint. Make them quite watery. Paint them in patches close to each other.

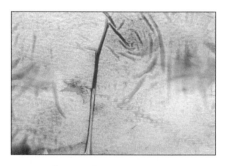

2. Before the paint has dried, cut a piece of plastic foodwrap larger than your painting. Then, lay it over the paint.

3. Use your fingers to move the paint under the foodwrap, to make patterns and blend the colors together.

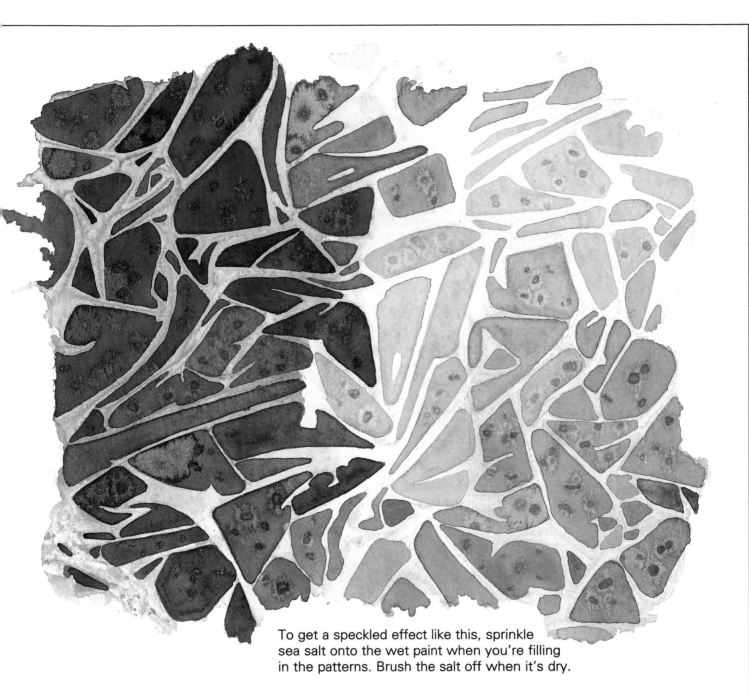

To get a speckled effect like this, sprinkle sea salt onto the wet paint when you're filling in the patterns. Brush the salt off when it's dry.

4. Leave the foodwrap on top of the paint and let the paint dry completely. Then, carefully peel off the foodwrap.

5. Use watercolor paints to fill in lots of the patterns left by the foodwrap. Leave a space around each shape.

6. Continue filling in the patterns using some strong colors and some paler ones. Leave some of the patterns unfilled.

Fall leaves

WATERCOLOR PAPER

1. Mix a little red and yellow watercolor paint to make orange. Paint it evenly across the bottom of the paper, like this.

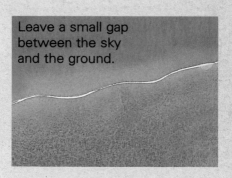

Leave a small gap between the sky and the ground.

2. Mix lots of Prussian blue watercolor paint with water. Paint across the top of the paper for the sky.

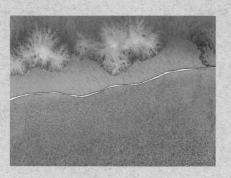

3. Before the sky has dried, dip a paintbrush into water, then let it drip onto the sky. The paint will spread a little.

4. Mix red and green acrylic paint to make brown. Drag your brush down several times to paint the tree trunk.

5. Add some branches in the same way, then use a thinner paintbrush to paint finer twigs at the ends of the branches.

6. When the paint is dry, use a brown oil pastel or wax crayon to draw wavy lines for the middle veins of the leaves.

7. Mix red and yellow watercolor paint to make shades of orange. Paint a leaf shape around each line.

8. Paint a few little leaves on the tree and some in the sky. This will make it look as if the leaves are blowing in the wind.

9. When all the leaves are dry, use a fine brush to paint lots of thin, dark brown lines on each of the large leaves.

This picture was painted on
rough watercolor paper
which gives the background
a grainy texture.

Tissue paper pond

TISSUE PAPER

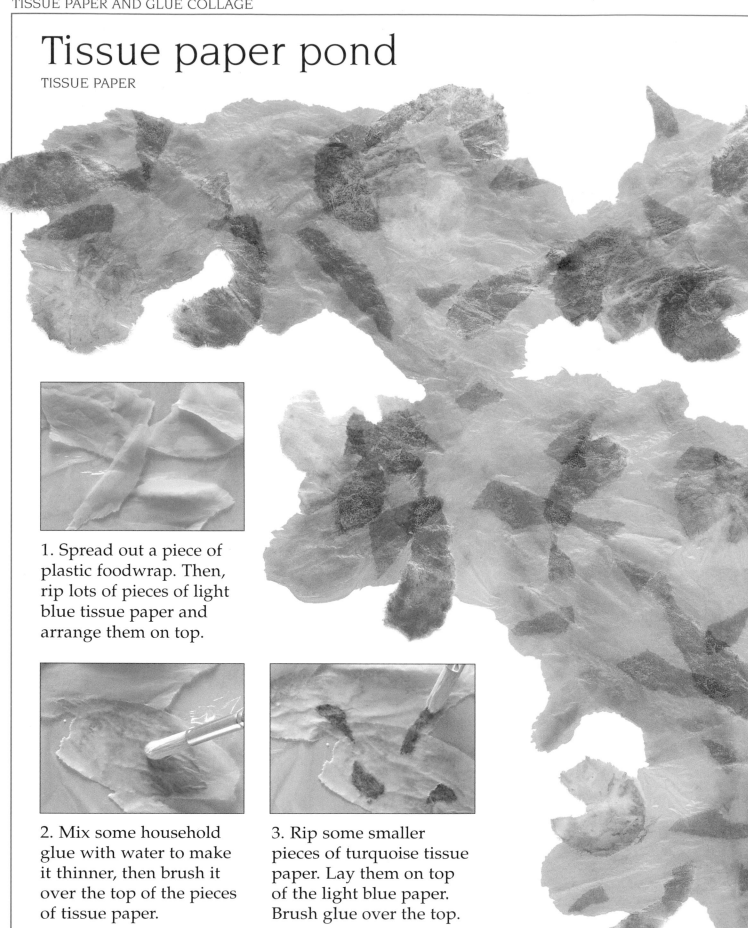

1. Spread out a piece of plastic foodwrap. Then, rip lots of pieces of light blue tissue paper and arrange them on top.

2. Mix some household glue with water to make it thinner, then brush it over the top of the pieces of tissue paper.

3. Rip some smaller pieces of turquoise tissue paper. Lay them on top of the light blue paper. Brush glue over the top.

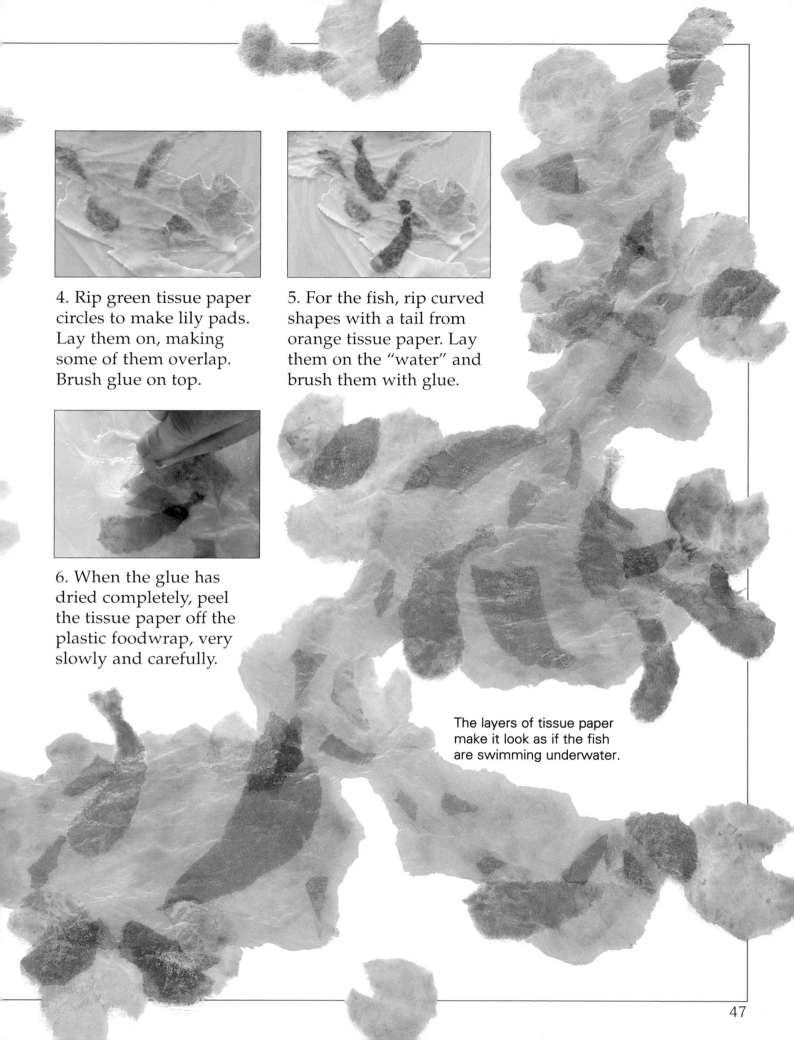

4. Rip green tissue paper circles to make lily pads. Lay them on, making some of them overlap. Brush glue on top.

5. For the fish, rip curved shapes with a tail from orange tissue paper. Lay them on the "water" and brush them with glue.

6. When the glue has dried completely, peel the tissue paper off the plastic foodwrap, very slowly and carefully.

The layers of tissue paper make it look as if the fish are swimming underwater.

Geometric prints

ANY PAPER

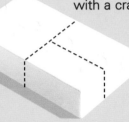

Be very careful when cutting with a craft knife.

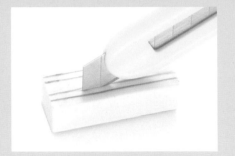

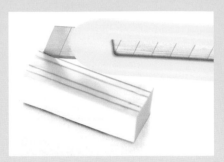

1. Use a craft knife to cut a long eraser in half. Then, cut one of the pieces of eraser in half lengthways.

2. Draw sets of parallel lines along the eraser. Then, holding the knife at an angle, make a clean cut along one line.

3. Turn the eraser around and cut along the other side of the line to make a groove. Cut the other line in the same way.

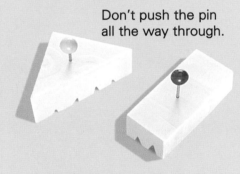

Don't push the pin all the way through.

4. Cut the corners off the other half of the eraser to make a triangle. Draw four lines on it, then cut along them as before.

5. Push a map pin or an ordinary pin into the back of both pieces of eraser. This makes them easier to hold when you print.

6. Wet a piece of sponge cloth, then squeeze out as much water as you can. Spread acrylic paint on it with the back of a spoon.

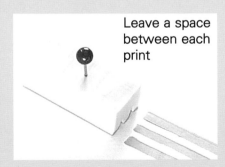

Leave a space between each print

7. Press the first eraser into the paint, then onto some paper. Press it in the paint again before you do another print.

8. Then, do a triangle print above each set of line prints. Repeat these rows of prints several times on your paper.

9. Cut a small square of eraser and print it between each triangle. Then, cut a line across another square of eraser and print it on top.

These geometric patterns were built up using erasers cut into different shapes.

Techniques for water

On the next four pages you will find different techniques for drawing and painting water. There are ideas for waves, rippling water and reflections of moonlight on water.

This photograph of a crashing wave shows different shapes, patterns and colors which can be found in water.

Soapy painting

Use a brush with stiff bristles.

1. Dip a brush into some blue watercolor paint. Then, move the bristles around on an old bar of soap.

2. Paint the soapy paint straight onto a piece of watercolor paper, moving the brush in a wavy pattern.

3. Dip the brush into a different shade of blue paint and then on the soap again. Paint more waves, overlapping them.

The soap helps to show the marks made by the paintbrush.

4. Paint a boat with thick red and blue watercolor paint. Add an outline with a fine felt-tip pen.

Oil pastel squiggles

1. Use a brown oil pastel to draw some rounded rocks on a piece of Bristol paper. Shade them in, like this.

2. Then, draw squiggles around the rocks with a turquoise oil pastel. Leave some spaces between them.

3. Add a dark blue pastel shadow beneath each rock and add more squiggles. Draw a turquoise reflection on each rock.

Painted ripples

1. Dampen a piece of watercolor paper with clean water. Then, paint it with blue watercolor paint, leaving some gaps.

2. When the paint is dry, paint wavy lines with a darker blue paint. Add some even darker ones with the tip of a brush.

51

More techniques for water
Sea collage

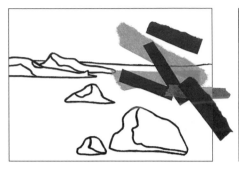

1. Draw some rocks on some thick cardboard and add a line for the horizon. Then, rip strips of blue tissue paper.

2. Paint the sky with blue acrylic paint. When the sky is dry, glue pieces of pale blue paper around the rocks for the sea.

3. Glue on some darker shades of blue paper. Rip paper shapes for rocks and glue them on. Add tissue paper shadows.

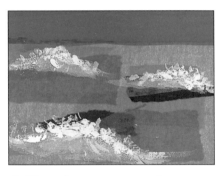

4. For the waves, glue on pieces of white tissue paper. Dab white acrylic or poster paint along the top of each wave.

5. Dip your brush in the paint again, then splatter it over the top of a wave by following steps 5 and 6 on page 73.

Wax resist reflections

1. Draw a moon with a white oil pastel on watercolor paper. It's shown here in yellow so that you can see it.

2. Add lots of short lines, starting about a third of the way down the paper. Make each line a little longer than the one before.

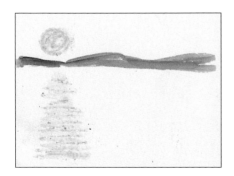

3. Use darkish blue watercolor paint to paint a line of distant hills between the moon and the lines on the water.

4. Then paint the sky and the water with yellow watercolor. Use a tissue to lift patches of paint off the sky, for clouds.

5. When the paint is dry, paint a strip of land. Paint a tree trunk, then dab on leaves with the tip of a brush and a sponge.

Ink and pastel pets

WATERCOLOR PAPER

The ink will run
on the paper.

1. Use a clean sponge or
a wide paintbrush to
wet a piece of
watercolor paper.

2. Dip a thick paintbrush
into some bright ink and
paint lines for the head,
ear, body, legs and tail.

3. While the ink is still
wet, use the tip of a brush
to add spots. Do one on
the head for the eye.

Fill in around the dog with
another color of ink.

4. When it's dry, outline
the body with a black felt-
tip pen. Add a nose, eyes
and lines on the paws.

5. Draw on a few dots
and hairs, too. Fill in the
nose and draw a collar
with chalk pastels.

54

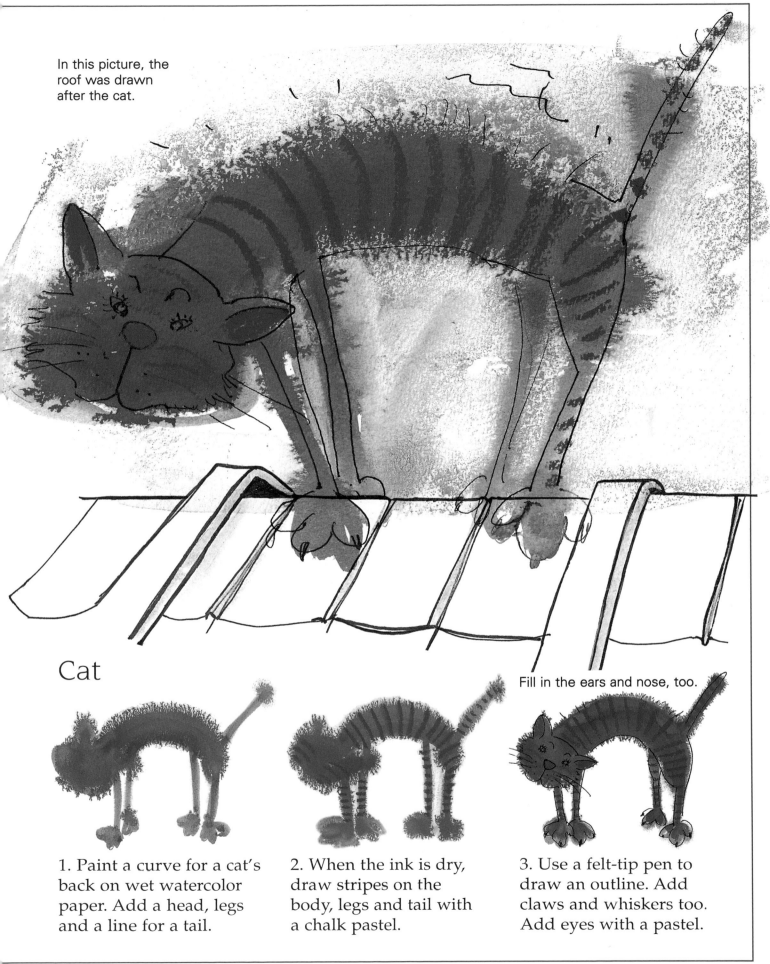

In this picture, the roof was drawn after the cat.

Cat

1. Paint a curve for a cat's back on wet watercolor paper. Add a head, legs and a line for a tail.

2. When the ink is dry, draw stripes on the body, legs and tail with a chalk pastel.

Fill in the ears and nose, too.

3. Use a felt-tip pen to draw an outline. Add claws and whiskers too. Add eyes with a pastel.

Blow-painted trees

THICK BRISTOL PAPER OR WATERCOLOR PAPER

 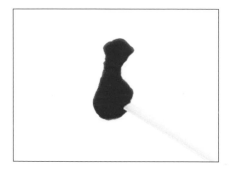 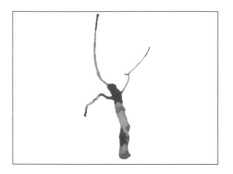

1. Dip a paintbrush into some bright ink and paint a thick blob for the tree trunk.

2. Blow through a drinking straw so that you extend the ink up the paper for the trunk.

3. Then, use the end of the straw to pull little lines of ink away from the trunk.

Drag little wisps of grass with the tip of a paintbrush.

56

You may need to add more ink.

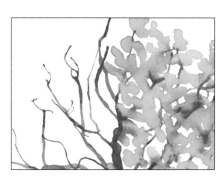

4. Blow the lines of ink to make the branches. Then, paint and blow more trees in the same way.

5. For the leaves, mix orange ink with water. Dab it over the branches again and again.

6. For the ground, mix more watery ink and paint it around the bottom of the trees.

Make the ink around the bottom of the trees darker than the areas in between them.

Domed buildings

THICK BRISTOL PAPER OR WATERCOLOR PAPER

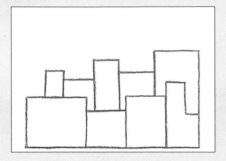

1. Use a pencil to draw several large rectangles on your paper. Make them different sizes.

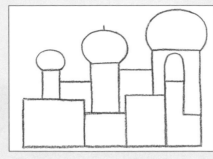

2. Add some domes and turrets. Make them different sizes and shapes, too.

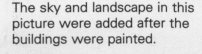

The sky and landscape in this picture were added after the buildings were painted.

3. Add lots of different shapes of windows, doorways, columns and arches to the buildings.

4. Use watercolor paints or inks to fill in the buildings. Leave a small gap between each part.

5. When the paint or ink is dry, fill in the domes with a gold felt-tip pen or gold paint.

6. Draw around some of the windows and add patterns to the buildings, with a gold pen.

Animal shapes
THIN CARDBOARD
Tessellating bird

1. Cut a corner off a square of thin cardboard then, tape the triangle along the top edge of the square, like this.

2. Cut the other bottom corner off the square and tape it along the top, so that the two triangles meet in the middle.

3. To make the beak, cut a long v-shape into the left-hand side. Tape the shape onto the triangle at the top.

Shapes like these, which fit together exactly to form repeating patterns, are called tessellations.

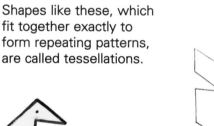

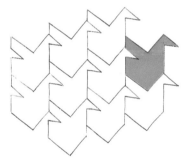

4. Draw around the bird shape. Then, move the shape so that the beak fits under the wing. Draw around it again.

5. Continue drawing around the shape so that you build up a pattern of birds which fit into each other on all sides.

These birds were painted with gouache, then outlined with a black felt-tip pen.

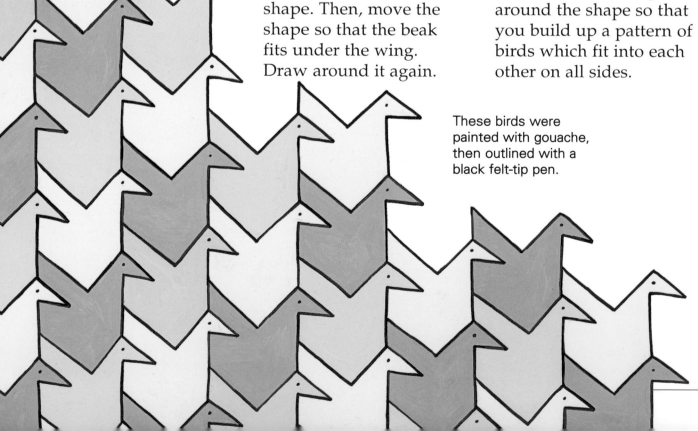

Transformations

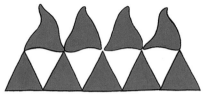

1. Draw a row of five tall triangles and fill them in. Add four triangles above them, making their sides curve slightly.

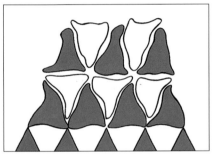

2. Draw three white curvy triangles in the spaces. Add more blue ones and white ones on top. Make the shapes curve, like this.

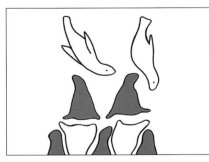

3. Draw two blue shapes which look like sitting seals. Then, draw several swimming seals. Add flippers and eyes.

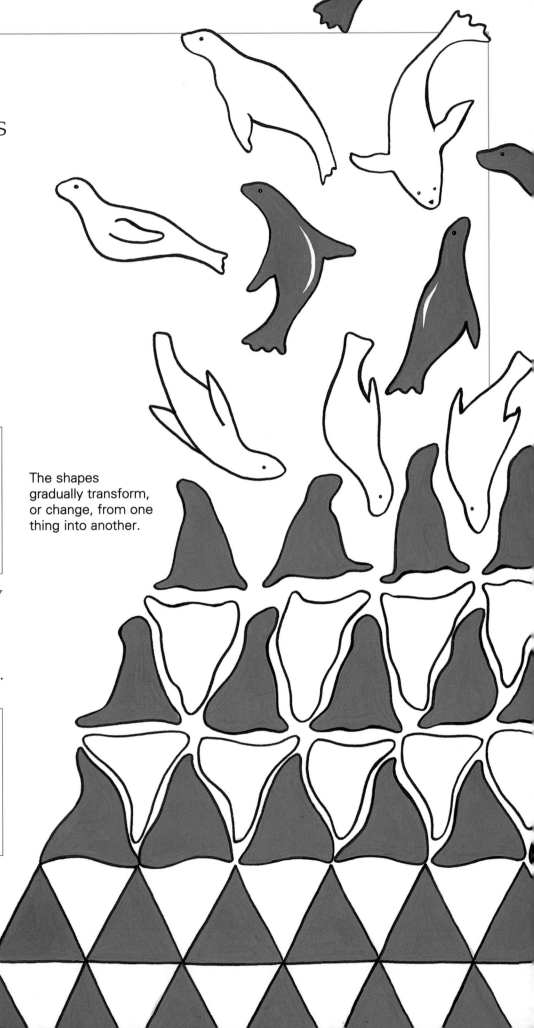

The shapes gradually transform, or change, from one thing into another.

Street scene

A PIECE OF THIN CARDBOARD

1. Make a pale apricot color by mixing white and orange acrylic paint. Brush it all over a large piece of cardboard.

2. When the paint has dried, paint a blue shape for the cab of a truck. Paint a brown tank and add dark blue wheels.

3. Use the apricot paint to add windows and headlights. Paint a curve on the tank, and two small tanks below. Let it dry.

To do a street scene like this, paint rough shapes for the signs, dog, and so on, before you do the outlines. Then draw some people.

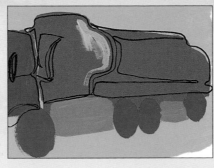

4. Without lifting your pen, outline the whole cab with a black felt-tip pen. You may need to go over some lines twice.

5. Continue the line onto the brown tank. Draw a shape for the flat part at the front of the tank, then outline the back part.

6. Continue the line around and around for the wheels and along the two small tanks under the truck, too.

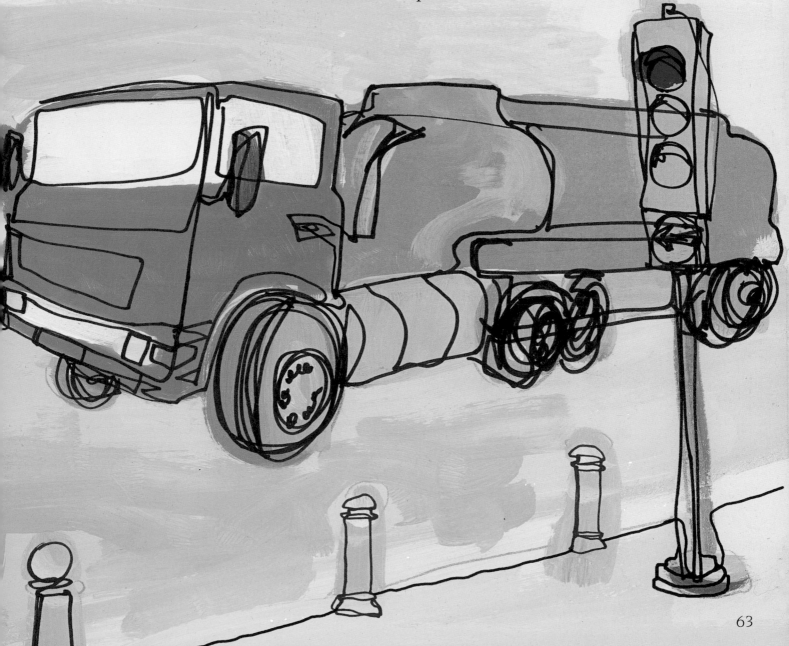

Techniques for fur

Some animals have long hairy fur, curly fur, or smooth skin. They can also be one color or have amazing patterned fur. Here are a few suggestions of different ways to draw animal fur:

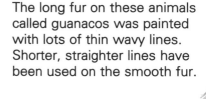

The long fur on these animals called guanacos was painted with lots of thin wavy lines. Shorter, straighter lines have been used on the smooth fur.

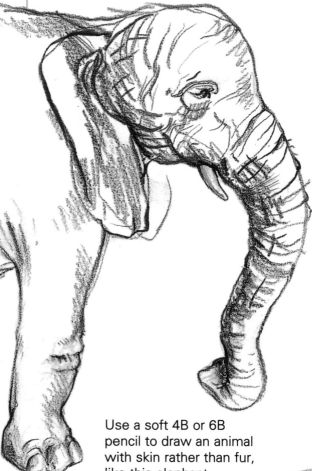

Use a soft 4B or 6B pencil to draw an animal with skin rather than fur, like this elephant.

Press harder and harder with a pencil for fur like this.

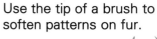

Use the tip of a brush to soften patterns on fur.

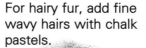

For hairy fur, add fine wavy hairs with chalk pastels.

The yellow of the giraffe fur above was painted first. The patterns were added when it had dried.

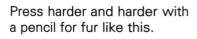

The spots and hair of this spotted fur were drawn on a patch of orange chalk pastel.

Pencil and paint

1. Use a soft 6B pencil to draw a lion's eyes, ears and nose. Add some curved lines for the mane.

2. Paint lines in shades of orange between the pencil lines, but don't put too much paint on your brush.

Add some shading down the side of the face and over the eyes when the paint is dry.

Chalk pastel leopard

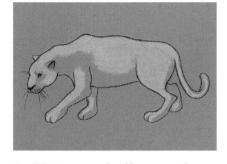

1. Use a pencil to draw a faint outline of a leopard on colored paper. Fill in its nose and eyes and add some long whiskers.

2. Using a chalk pastel, fill in areas on the leopard's head, along the neck and back, and down the legs and tail.

3. Use a darker pastel to fill in shadows under the chin and on the tail, legs and tummy. Smudge the pastel with a finger.

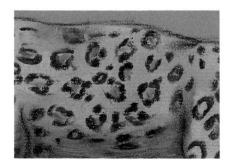

4. Add spots on the head, back, tail and legs. Then, outline the leopard and its eyes and nose with a black pastel.

More techniques for fur

Watercolor seal

1. Draw the outline of a seal's body with a pencil on watercolor paper. Add the flippers.

2. Fill in your outline with blue watercolor paint. Use Prussian blue if you have it.

3. Before the paint has dried, lift off a line of paint along the body with a tissue or a dry brush.

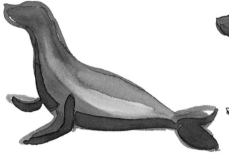

4. Paint darker blue lines for shadows along the neck, flippers, tummy, and on the tail.

The pen lines will bleed a little.

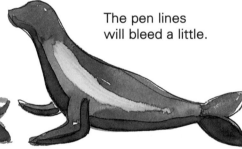

5. Before the lines have dried, outline the seal with a water-based felt-tip pen.

6. Use the pen to add an eye, ear and nose. Draw some dots on the chin and add long whiskers.

The different shades of blue help to make the seals' fur look sleek and smooth.

This dog's tail has been printed more than once. It makes it look as if it's wagging.

Dragged paint dogs

Make sure you have lots of paint on your brush.

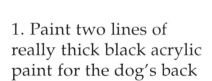

1. Paint two lines of really thick black acrylic paint for the dog's back and head.

2. Use the edge of a piece of cardboard to drag the paint downward to make the head and body.

3. Use the corner of the cardboard to drag the paint to make the ears, legs and tail.

Use a ballpoint or felt-tip pen.

4. When the paint is dry, draw wavy lines under the head and body. Add lines to the ears and feet.

5. Draw a curved line for a collar around the dog's neck with a bright chalk pastel or oil pastel.

6. Then, use a craft knife to scratch vertical lines into the paint on the dog's head and body.

Wet paper watercolor

WATERCOLOR PAPER

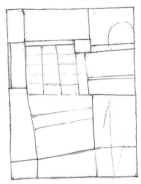

1. Do a plan on some scrap paper before you start. Draw a rectangle and fill it with shapes, like this.

2. Paint a rectangle of watercolor paper with clean water. Following your plan, fill in the main shapes with pale colors.

3. When the paint has dried, fill some of the shapes with a stronger color. Paint patterns in some of the shapes.

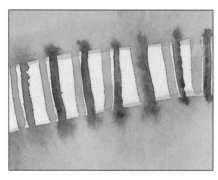

4. While the paint is still wet, add small lines in different colors, letting the paints bleed into each other.

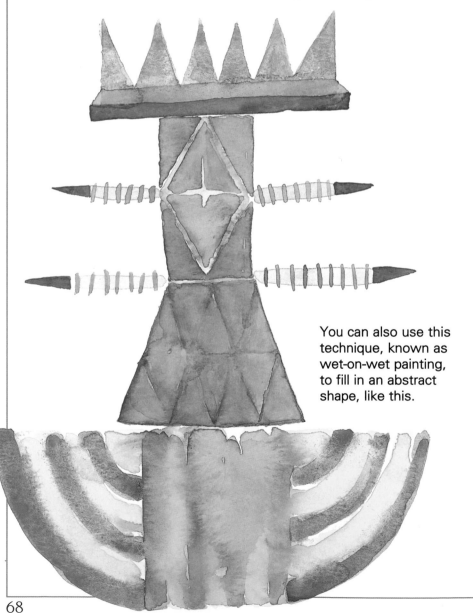

You can also use this technique, known as wet-on-wet painting, to fill in an abstract shape, like this.

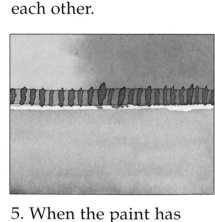

5. When the paint has dried, paint some more little lines. The colors won't bleed as they did when the paint was wet.

Town collage

BRISTOL PAPER OR THIN CARDBOARD

1. Make a rough plan for your collage on a piece of scrap paper. Mark on the position of roads, a park, buildings, cars, and so on.

2. On a large piece of paper or cardboard, paint the shapes which are the roads on your plan, with acrylic or poster paint.

3. For the park, rip pieces of light-colored paper from old magazines and glue them. Add green paper for grass.

4. Fill in the areas for the buildings with dark pieces of paper. Rip shapes for the buildings and add some windows.

5. For the cars, rip a shape for the body, with wheel arches ripped out. Glue two wheels behind and windows on top.

6. For a cat, rip the body from magazine paper which has a texture on it. Glue on paws. Cut out an eye and glue it on, too.

The shapes in this collage were glued on at different angles to give it a topsy-turvy effect.

7. For the people, rip all the parts of the body and the clothes. Glue the pieces together, then glue them onto the collage.

Wax resist fish and butterflies

BRISTOL PAPER

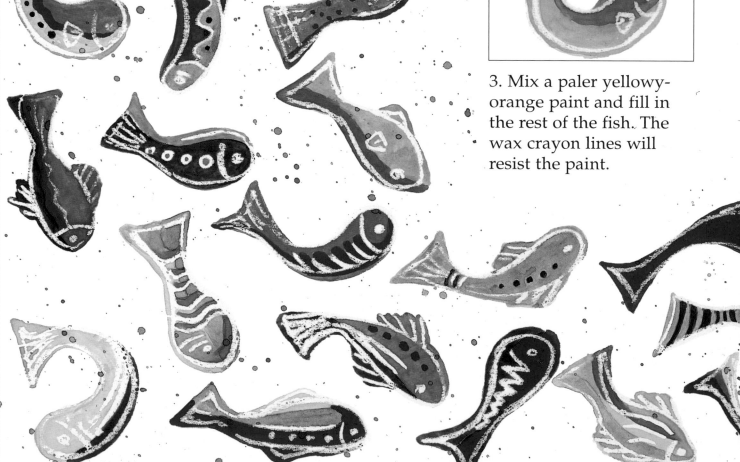

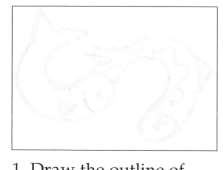

1. Draw the outline of some fish with a pale yellow wax crayon. Add eyes, fins and some patterns on the bodies.

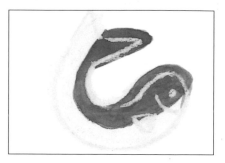

2. Mix some orange watercolor paint and paint part of each fish. Don't worry if you overlap the outline a little.

3. Mix a paler yellowy-orange paint and fill in the rest of the fish. The wax crayon lines will resist the paint.

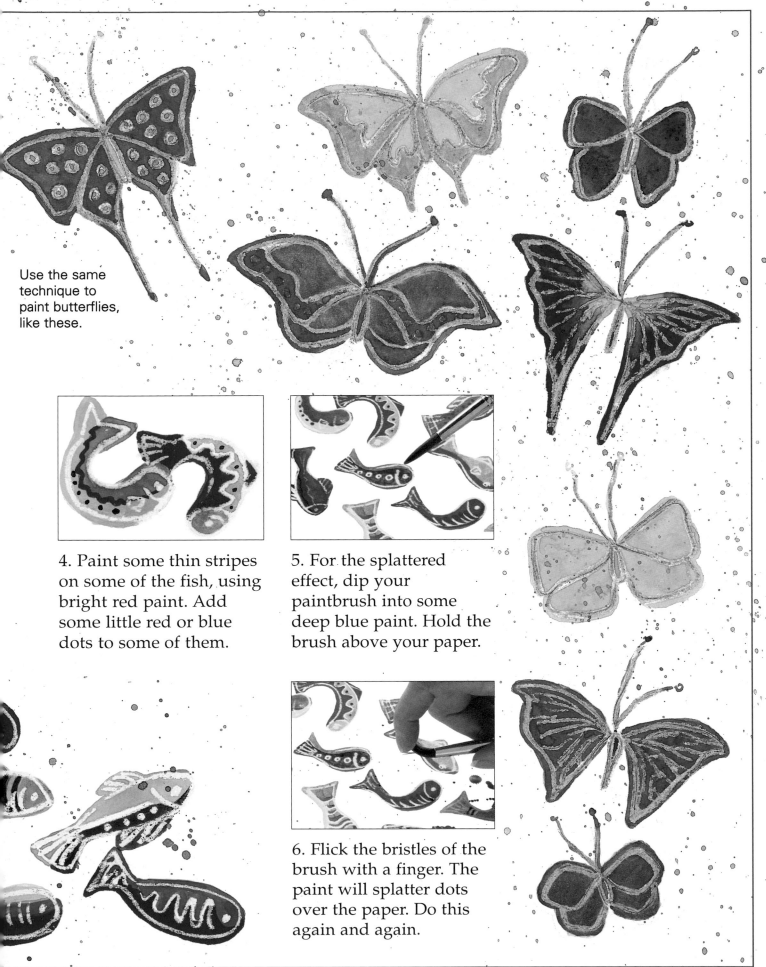

Use the same technique to paint butterflies, like these.

4. Paint some thin stripes on some of the fish, using bright red paint. Add some little red or blue dots to some of them.

5. For the splattered effect, dip your paintbrush into some deep blue paint. Hold the brush above your paper.

6. Flick the bristles of the brush with a finger. The paint will splatter dots over the paper. Do this again and again.

Cityscape

WHITE OR COLORED PAPER OR THIN CARDBOARD

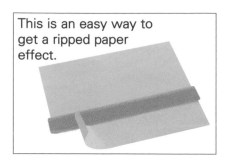

This is an easy way to get a ripped paper effect.

1. For the road, lay a ruler on a piece of paper. Press firmly on the ruler and rip the paper along its edge.

2. Glue the road along the bottom of a large piece of paper. Rip another piece, with an angle at one end, and glue it on.

3. For the buildings, rip rectangles from lots of different kinds of paper. Rip tower shapes on one end of some of them.

Use different types of paper, such as brown wrapping paper, or old envelopes.

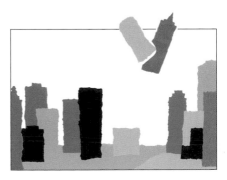

4. Arrange the rectangles of paper along the road, then glue them on. Overlap some of them to get a 3-D effect.

5. Cut out and glue lots of windows on some of the buildings. Glue some strips of white tissue paper on some, too.

6. Draw an outline around a few of the buildings with a black felt-tip pen. Draw windows on some of them, too.

Draw some tiny cars. This helps to make the buildings look massive.

Sheep on a hill

THICK BRISTOL OR WATERCOLOR PAPER

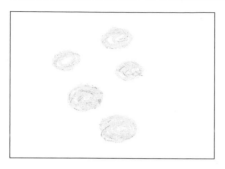

1. Use a white oil pastel to draw ovals for the sheep's bodies. They are shown here in yellow so that you can see them.

2. Use the pastel to draw some horizontal lines in front of the ovals. Add some thinner lines between the sheep, too.

3. Then, brush a rectangle of watery purple and pink watercolor paint on top. The pastel resists the paint.

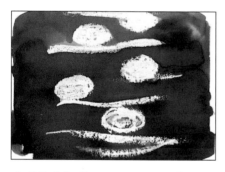

4. Hold the paper and gently tilt it from side to side so that the colors blend together. Then, leave it to dry.

5. Mix some dark blue paint or ink and paint a little oval on each sheep's body for a head. Add four stick legs, too.

6. Dip your paintbrush into thick white paint and splatter the snow by following steps 5 and 6 on page 73.

Other ideas

Draw flowers with white and yellow oil pastels. Paint green watercolor on top, then scratch the stalks with a craft knife.

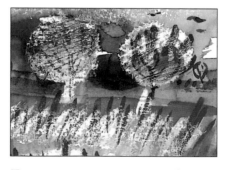

Draw trees, grass and clouds in white. Paint over the sky, trees and grass. When the paint's dry, scratch across the pastel.

Draw buildings with oil pastels. Add white roads and hills. Paint over them with blue, then sponge thick white paint on top.

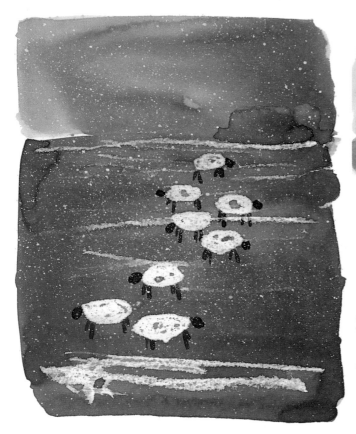

The cloud effect in the sky happens when you tilt the paper and the colors blend together.

The tufts of grass were painted in a slightly darker green once the background had dried.

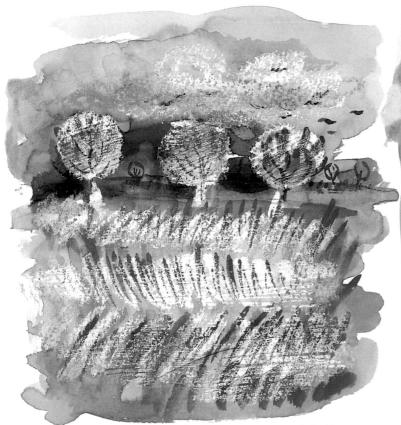

If you scratch the paint away with a craft knife, the pastel and paper are revealed underneath.

The windows were painted over the pastel, which resisted the paint, making uneven lines.

Techniques for feathers

Birds' feathers can be speckled or spotted, striped or plain. On this double page there are a few techniques for painting and drawing birds and feathers.

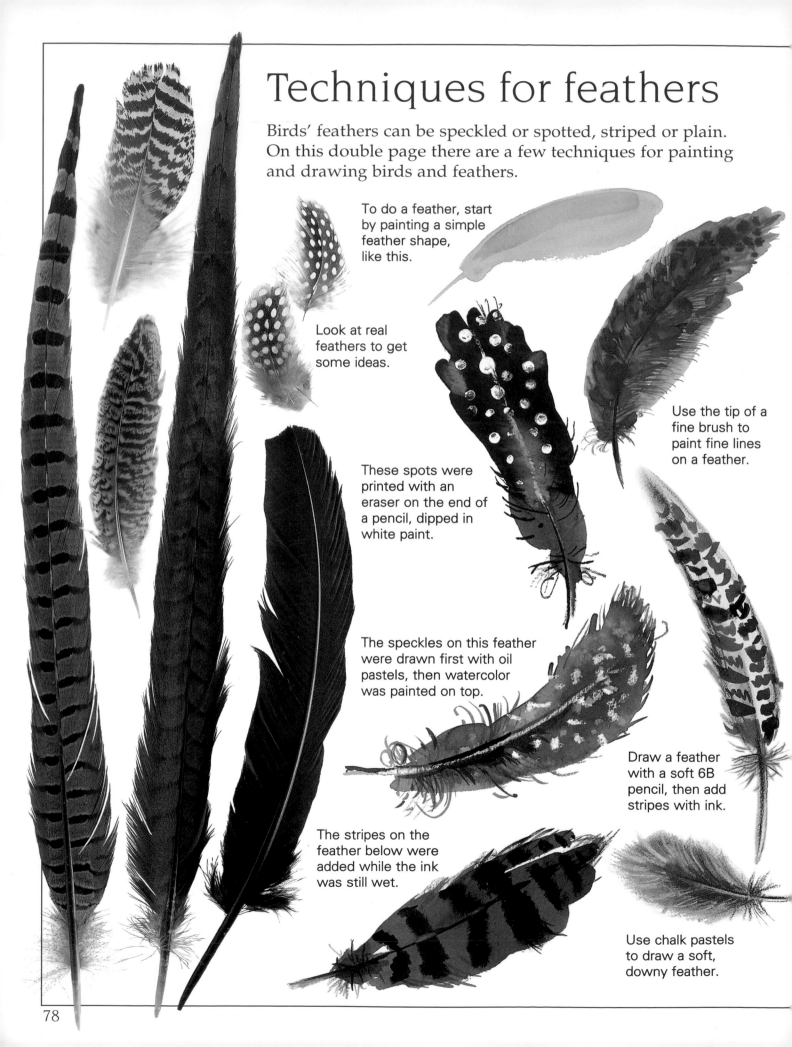

To do a feather, start by painting a simple feather shape, like this.

Look at real feathers to get some ideas.

Use the tip of a fine brush to paint fine lines on a feather.

These spots were printed with an eraser on the end of a pencil, dipped in white paint.

The speckles on this feather were drawn first with oil pastels, then watercolor was painted on top.

Draw a feather with a soft 6B pencil, then add stripes with ink.

The stripes on the feather below were added while the ink was still wet.

Use chalk pastels to draw a soft, downy feather.

Pheasant

1. Paint the body using watery brown watercolor paint. Go over the head, tail, tummy and legs with a darker brown.

2. While the paint is wet, add black and brown dots to the tail and tummy. Paint dark areas on the head, beak and neck.

3. Paint around the eye with red paint. Use a thin felt-tip pen to outline the body, adding feathers to the wing and tail.

Spotted woodpecker

1. Paint a thick black line for the head, back and tail. Then use finer lines for the rest of the body.

2. Paint a line on the tummy with watery ink. Fingerpaint spots on the tail with acrylic paint.

3. Fill in the body with a peach-colored chalk pastel. Add markings on the back and wing.

4. Draw a red chalk patch on the head and tummy. Smudge the pastel a little with your finger.

This woodpecker was painted in ink. The branch was drawn with a 6B pencil.

Swimming turtles

WATERCOLOR PAPER

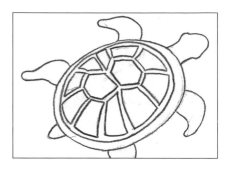

1. Use a blue pencil to draw a faint outline of a turtle's shell. Add a head, flippers, a tail and markings on the shell.

2. Paint markings on the shell with turquoise watercolor paint. Before the shapes dry, add a few dots. The paint will run.

3. Fill in the head, tail and flippers with turquoise paint. Then, add dots of paint to them before they have dried.

To get this effect around the turtle, the painting was covered with plastic foodwrap.

This is the effect you get when salt crystals are sprinkled onto the wet paint.

4. Paint the paper around the turtle with clean water. While the paper is still wet, add patches of green and turquoise paint.

5. Either sprinkle salt crystals over the wet paint, or lay a layer of plastic foodwrap over the painting. Leave it to dry.

6. Then, when the paint has dried completely, brush off all the salt crystals, or pull off the plastic foodwrap.

Pastel landscape
ANY TYPE OF YELLOW OR BEIGE PAPER

1. Using a pencil, draw a plan for your pastel landscape on a large piece of yellow or beige colored paper.

2. Make the pencil lighter with an eraser. Then, fill in the background with a mustard-colored chalk pastel. Fill in some shapes.

3. Draw a tree trunk with a brown pastel. Add green leaves, then add shadows and highlights with dark and light green pastels.

4. For the buildings, fill in the main part with chalk pastels, leaving gaps for the window frames and door, then fill them in.

5. Draw green stems and leaves for the sunflowers. Add darker lines. Use yellow for the flowers and add orange on top.

6. Draw a white oval for the fountain. Outline the boy and the dog in blue, then fill them in. Fill in the water last of all.

7. Use the mustard chalk pastel to go over parts of the background again, around each of the things you have drawn.

To stop pastels from smudging, you can fix them with fixative spray or hair spray.

Cloud people
WATERCOLOR PAPER

Wipe the brush on a paper towel after each shape.

1. Mix some watery dark blue watercolor paint, then use a thick brush to paint a large patch of color, like this.

2. Brush some of the paint away from the patch to make the shapes for the clown's hat and collar. Let the patch dry a little.

3. Then, using a clean, dry brush, lift off a curve of paint for the clown's chin and shapes for the nose and eyebrows.

4. Leave the paint to dry completely, then use dark blue paint to add shadows under the nose and chin.

5. Add lines for the eyebrows and the eyes. Then, paint a line for the side of the face and some curved lines on the collar.

84

This character is an admiral with a long nose, a curly moustache and a beard. Lines and dots show his uniform.

Add a crown and hair ribbons to create a princess.

You can lift off paint to make the brim of a hat or a bulbous nose.

6. Use a thin brush and the dark blue paint to paint the outline of the hat. Add two small circles for bells.

7. Paint pupils in each eye. Then, add a little line above and below each eye, for the clown's face paint.

8. Paint two lines for the lips. Add little lines at each side of the mouth, to make the clown look as if it is grinning.

9. Paint two curved lines at the side of the face for the ears. Then, add several curved lines for ruffles on the collar.

Scratched patterns

BRISTOL PAPER

This patch was scratched with random shapes and patterns.

1. Use different oil pastels to draw patches of color on a piece of Bristol paper. Make sure that the patches join together.

2. Mix a little water with black acrylic paint, but don't make it too thin. Cover the oil pastel completely with the paint.

3. Leave the paint until it is almost dry. Then, use a screwdriver to scratch lines, revealing the pastel underneath.

4. Scratch several more lines down the paint, then scratch lines across to make a large grid. Scratch a border, too.

5. Draw a simple outline of a bird in part of the grid. Add curved lines for feathers, a wing, an eye and a beak.

6. If you make a mistake, paint some of the black acrylic paint on top and let it dry a little before scratching it again.

Giraffe collage

A LARGE PIECE OF THIN CARDBOARD

Don't glue these areas yet.

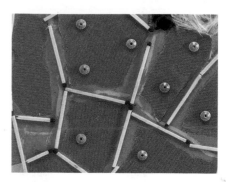

1. Glue a piece of brown butcher paper onto some cardboard. Then, rip another piece of paper. Glue it across the bottom.

2. Cut out a giraffe's body and legs. Cut a head from corrugated cardboard. Glue the pieces to the background, like this.

3. Rip lots of patches from brown paper and glue them onto the body. Glue matchsticks around them. Add beads or dried beans.

4. Glue fluffy feathers or lots of pieces of yarn down the neck for the mane. Glue long feathers over the top.

5. Wrap black yarn around each hoof and glue on things like matchsticks, feathers and pieces of shiny paper.

6. For the giraffe's antlers, twist the wire off an old clothespin. Glue a large, dried seed or bean onto the end of each pin.

Make birds to glue around the giraffe by ripping a paper body and wing. Join them with a paper fastener.

7. For eyes, glue together things such as feathers, dried plants and buttons. Glue them on, then glue the rest of the body down.

Don't worry if you don't
have exactly the objects
shown on this picture -
use whatever you can find.

The tail was tucked
underneath the body
before the body was
glued down.

Pencil bugs
ANY PAPER WITH A SMOOTH SURFACE

1. Use a pencil with a soft lead (a 6B pencil is ideal) to draw a simple outline of an insect on your paper.

2. Shade the insect's body, making it darker close to the edges. Fill in the head and legs. Add any spots or patterns, too.

3. Rub lines across your drawing with an eraser to smudge the pencil a little. Rub the lines in different directions.

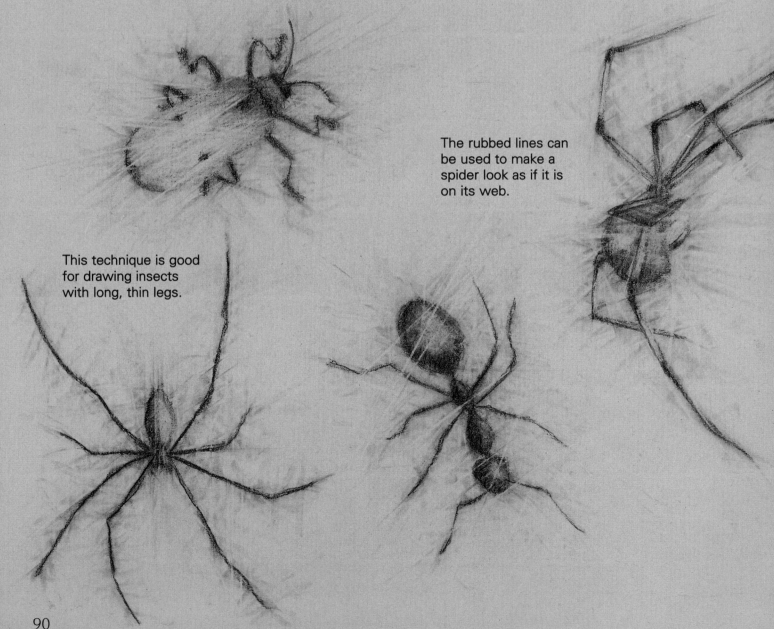

The rubbed lines can be used to make a spider look as if it is on its web.

This technique is good for drawing insects with long, thin legs.

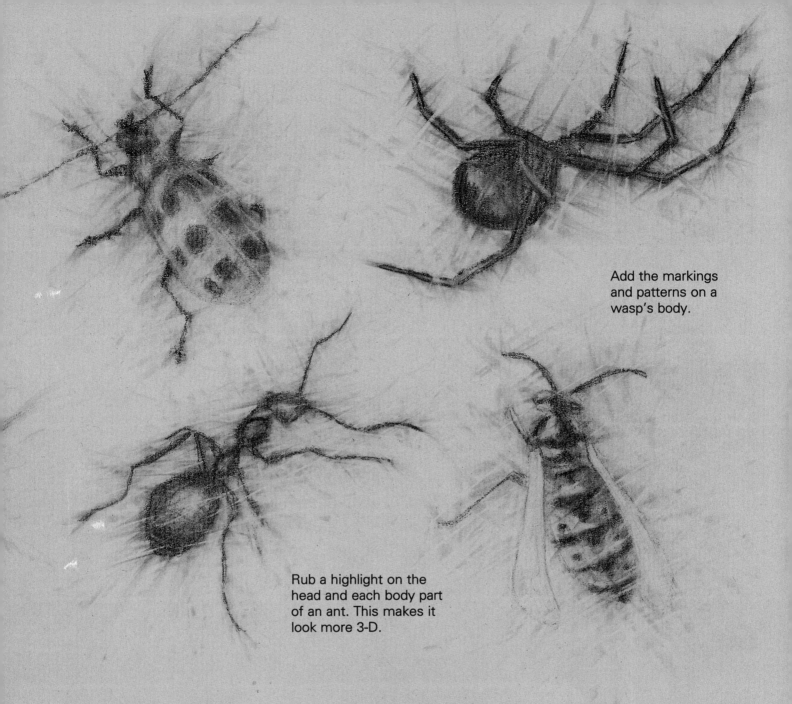

Add the markings and patterns on a wasp's body.

Rub a highlight on the head and each body part of an ant. This makes it look more 3-D.

4. Use a harder pencil, such as a 2B, to draw over the insect again. Add shading and details to it too.

5. Rub lines over the drawing again, but be more careful this time. You just want to smudge the lines a little.

6. Then, use the eraser to rub away some of the pencil shading to create a shiny highlighted patch on the insect's body.

More ideas

Over the next four pages there are lots more ideas for using the techniques in this book. Turn back to the pages which are mentioned to find out how they were done.

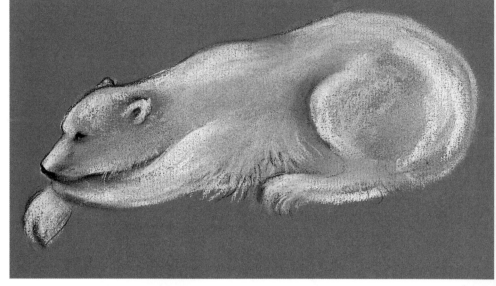

This polar bear was drawn with chalk pastels, like the leopard on page 65.

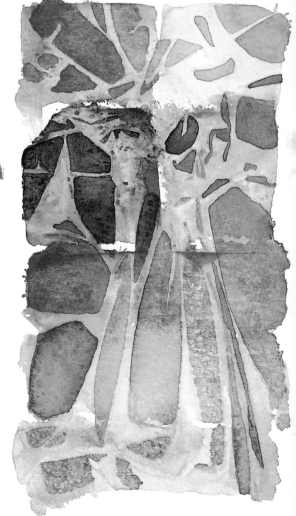

These birds were made with ripped paper from old magazines (see pages 70-71).

This pattern was created with plastic foodwrap (see pages 42-43).

These buildings were based on the domed ones on pages 58-59.

This is another idea for using the wet-on-wet technique (see pages 68-69).

These insects use the same technique as the fish on pages 72-73.

This dog was painted with inks and chalk pastels (see pages 54-55).

93

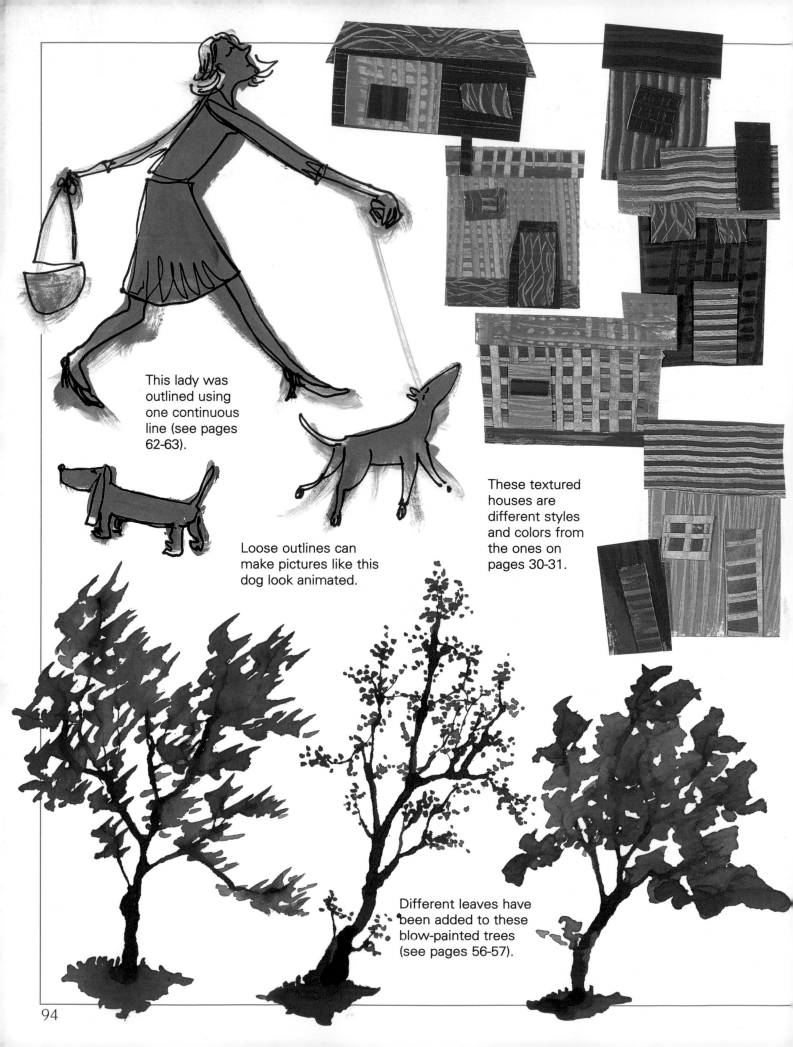

This lady was outlined using one continuous line (see pages 62-63).

Loose outlines can make pictures like this dog look animated.

These textured houses are different styles and colors from the ones on pages 30-31.

Different leaves have been added to these blow-painted trees (see pages 56-57).

This colorful picture is a variation of the doodle painting on page 40.

The background for this frog was created using plastic foodwrap (see pages 80-81).

The background for this Western sunset was created by dragging paint with pieces of cardboard (see page 12).

To make a snail collage, rip pieces of tissue paper (see pages 46-47).

Details on this painted giraffe were added with pastels (see page 65) and pen.

Index

Acknowledgements

Every effort has been made to trace the copyright holders of the material in this book. If any rights have been omitted, the publishers offer their sincere apologies and will rectify this in any subsequent edition following notification. The publishers are grateful to the following organisations and individuals for their contributions and permission to reproduce material. Page 20 Vincent van Gogh, 'Olive Trees' (1889) © Minneapolis Institute of Arts, MN, USA, The William Hood DunWoody Fund/ Bridgeman Images. Page 34 J.M.W: Turner, 'Rain, Steam, and Speed - The Great Western Railway' (1884) © National Gallery, London, UK/Bridgeman Images. Page 50 Waves © Digital Vision. Page 64 Guanacos - Ian Jackson.